"In my view, con
problems. People a
their pocket and bu, .
solve their problem. Entrepreneurship is inherent in all of us – in very different ways. And if we - like me - believe that there is a God who conceived and created this world, then as "The Great Entrepreneur" he also planted an entrepreneurial gene in each of us. This book is a motivational trigger for us all to discover our entrepreneurial gene."

Dr Jules Dubowy, Thank God it's Monday

"I grew up in poverty, orphaned at a young age and experienced first hand struggle in my life. Becoming an entrepreneur taught me that there is no shame in being born poor, disadvantaged or uneducated, but you don't have to stay there. I highly recommend 'The Great Entrepreneur'"

Jeff Lestz, Founder of Genistar

"The Great Entrepreneur will motivate and inspire you to launch the business idea you've been dreaming about. It tells the truth about the God-given gift of entrepreneurship, and how this can be and should be harnessed to solve the world's greatest problems."

Allie Amoroso, Rose Woman's Foundation

"Matt Bird has immense knowledge and experience in the fields of entrepreneurship and economics. This book embodies who he is as a positive change agent in the world. If you want to be a greater change agent and are looking for actionable strategies, I highly recommend The Great Entrepreneur. It will change you, the people around you and the world .....Thank me later!"

Peter Low, Chief Multiplying Officer at 100X

"It takes God and grit to build a business! Matt Bird has both and in this excellent book - The Great Entrepreneur - he helps us to achieve greater impact."

Sir Peter Vardy,
The Vardy Foundation & Family Office

"Fasten your seat belt. This book calls everyone into action. If God is The Great Entrepreneur, we cannot be couch potatoes."

Cris Auditore, CEO of Vasari Ventures

"Read this book and change the way you read the Bible: it will energise your daily life! Entrepreneurship is about making a real impact."

Luc Maroni,
Founder of the "Do what you want!"
School of Entrepreneurs

"The Great Entrepreneur is a critical and timely revelation of the creative and industrious nature of God. It provides hope for a generation that is increasingly disillusioned by promises to tackle the cost-of-living crisis. Matt Bird is an serial entrepreneur who understands how to help other entrepreneurs while walking and in hand with the great entrepreneur Himself!"

Bishop Wayne Malcolm,
iCan Community Church UK

The Great Entrepreneur

PublishU Ltd

www.PublishU.com

Thanks to the world's entrepreneurs who are helping beat the cost-of-living crisis.

Contents

Introduction

First published in The Times newspaper
5 November, 2022

It feels like the weekly shopping gets more expensive every time you check out. And the recent announcement that in the past twelve months the cost of living has increased by ten per cent, explains why.

Most people who can absorb these increases feel the strain for children, relatives and neighbours. For those who cannot, this creates unimaginable stress, an assault on well-being and potentially much worse.

No matter how much tax a government takes or how successful charities might be at fundraising, they'll never be able to run enough welfare programmes to meet every community's needs and, some would say, nor should they.

The only lasting and dignified solution to financial hardship is the creation of new jobs and new enterprises. As the saying goes, "If you give a person a fish you feed them for a day, but if you teach them how to fish you feed them for life." Food banks and food parcels are wonderful acts of human generosity, but they don't solve the continuing challenge of people experiencing financial difficulty.

In the midst of a global cost-of-living crisis, the need has never been greater to help people to start new businesses as a lasting solution to financial hardship.

This isn't just an opportunity for people without work to start a money-making business that provides for them and their family. It's also a chance for people with a job but who are finding it increasingly difficult to make ends meet. Starting a money-making "side hustle" can supplement their income.

As I wrote in this column in January last year: "We need an outbreak of something more powerful than a virus: the spirit of enterprise. It's time for new business enterprises that can create value and jobs to replace the hundreds of thousands being lost."

In the same way, today we need something more powerful than the cost-of-living crisis: the spirit of enterprise to start thousands of business enterprises that create income for people who are struggling.

The feedback I received from last year's column inspired me to write a seven-session course — 'The Spirit of Enterprise' — that enables churches to help people in financial hardship to start a business. The course was published as a book in six languages and is now being used by thirty-four churches in seven countries to help people lift themselves out of poverty.

Churches are understanding the vision of enterprise as a force for good: they're not only running the course but developing other enterprise initiatives to meet the needs of their communities. One example is the Bridge Church, in Birmingham, which has bought a community building to run the course. It will also launch a hub under the auspices of 'NAYBA,' the global social enterprise I run, to support emerging entrepreneurs with mentors, office space and other resources.

The Pope met last week with a group of entrepreneurs from Spain, encouraging them to "continue to creatively transform the face of the economy, so that it may be more attentive to ethical principle" as well as to "not forget that its activity is at the service of the human being, not just of the few, but of all, especially the poor."

A powerful example of what the Pope was speaking about is the 'Benefact Group' of financial services in the UK. It's wholly owned by the 'Benefact Trust,' which donates one hundred per cent of profits to achieving good in communities. It recently celebrated the landmark of having given away one hundred million pounds and has awarded 'NAYBA' a major grant to address the cost-of-living crisis by scaling up the 'Spirit of Enterprise' course through churches in the UK and Ireland.

This week, I'll speak at the 'Great Entrepreneur' conference in France to inspire leaders to use enterprise practically to bring about the transformation of families and neighbourhoods.

I proposed this subject because if an entrepreneur is defined as someone who takes a risk to create something out of nothing, then that makes God "the Great Entrepreneur." The Bible teaches that when nothing existed, God created a world that was good and took the risk to create human beings to look after it. As people, created in the likeness of an entrepreneurial God, we'll have the spirit of enterprise within us.

There's a clear opportunity across the UK, Ireland, mainland Europe and the rest of the world to inspire practical hope through the God-given gift of enterprise.

So, what are we waiting for? Government and charity will never solve poverty; only enterprise and business can bring about the lasting transformation of communities. Let's encourage an outbreak of the spirit of enterprise to give people the inspiration and resources to start new businesses.

Matt Bird

Business & Social Entrepreneur

matt@matt-bird.com

Chapter 1

The Great Entrepreneur

Enterprise is Who God is

When do you remember first doing something entrepreneurial? I remember mine: I was a teenager and it was school lunch break.

The lunchbox that my lovely mum prepared for me each day contained good food but not always the posh stuff that other kids had, such as packets of crisps. The family budget didn't quite run to those luxuries. There was always a Marmite sandwich and an apple and the one "treat" was a bar of chocolate because my dad had the fortune of working for a food business that had a large confectionery division. He visited the staff shop once a week and alongside other more staple food supplies, he'd buy a box of chocolate bars.

Back to the lunch break: Barney, the most popular boy in the class, leaned across and looked in my lunchbox. When he saw the bar of chocolate, he immediately made me a cash offer, which I accepted (especially as it was more than twice what my dad paid for it).

The next day, I managed to squeeze a couple extra chocolate bars in my lunchbox before leaving home. When I opened it, Barney immediately asked if he could buy two bars and a quick exchange followed. Given Barney's popularity — and other kids' desire to be like him — I quickly sold the extra chocolate bars I had too.

The following day, I brought an entire box of chocolate bars to school in my sports bag. I opened the bag at break time and sold the entire stock in a matter of minutes. Now I had a supply problem! I talked with my dad and asked if he could go into the staff shop a few times a week because I was going to need a box of chocolate bars every day.

In the midst of all this, the other kids in my class were rising very early every morning to cycle to the local newsagents to collect a bag of papers to deliver. They had to do this come rain, ice or snow or lose their job, and were remunerated five pounds per week. I was grateful to be earning more in one day than they did in an entire week and I didn't need to get up at crazy hours and face the English weather!

I didn't realise at the time, but this was my first experience of being an entrepreneur. I was learning about pricing and margins, supply chains, the value of "celebrity" ambassadors, how to work smarter not harder and much more besides.

Enterprise is What God Does

Enterprise is at the heart of who we are because it's at the heart of who God is. Please allow me to explain:

If an entrepreneur is someone who takes the risk to create something out of nothing, then that makes God the Great Entrepreneur. The first chapter of the Bible explains that in the beginning was God and nothing else. He spoke and created something out of nothing. He created the shape of the universe and then the content of the universe and then He took a big risk! He created men and women and gave us responsibility over all that He had made. It was a big, big risk and there are times when it's paid off for Him and times when it hasn't. God is the Greatest Entrepreneur.

Genesis explains we're created in the likeness of God. So, if God is the Great Entrepreneur and we're created in His likeness, then we all have the spirit of enterprise within us. It doesn't matter if we think we're a particularly creative person or not, we're fundamentally enterprising. Like God, we're creative, innovative, generative and productive. It's in our nature because it's in God's nature.

We not only have a God-given likeness of creativity and enterprise but we have a God-given mandate to "be fruitful and increase" (Genesis 1:28). We were given responsibility for husbandry to care for and to cultivate all of creation, including the fish of the sea, the birds of the air, the livestock on the ground and every seed-bearing plant. We're not only made but we're mandated to steward and manage and to be fruitful, increase and multiply. These are the core attributes of great entrepreneurs.

All this enterprise is within the context of love, relationship and community. Genesis shows us that God is love because He is One and He is Plural. Genesis says that before anything existed God was; that the Spirit of God was hovering and that when God spoke His "Word," creation came into being.

So there we have it: from the beginning of the Bible, we see a shadow of the revelation of God as trinity — One in Three and Three in One. As the revelation of who God is grows, we understand that the Father loves the Son and the Son loves the Father, and they send the Holy Spirit into the world. There in the Godhead we see a mutual love, preference for the other and sacrifice. We've been made in the likeness of God, which means we're also made for love, relationships and community. Whatever we believe or don't believe about God; we can only become all that God wants us to be in love, relationship and community with others.

Weak theology is built on a single biblical text. There are quite a few bits of theology out there in the "Christian scene" that are built on a pretty tenuous basis and on a single biblical text. Strong theology, however, is built on a biblical theme that runs throughout the Bible from beginning to end.

A theology of enterprise is a great example of good theology because it's built on a theme that runs throughout the Bible from beginning to end. Sadly, this theme has generally not been mined and explored. The revelation of Godly enterprise sits there alongside other great revelations like that God is Love.

Abraham is looked at as the great father of faith. Those people whose lives are focused on developing words and philosophy about God, describe the "Abrahamic Covenant." This is the initiative of God's promise to Abraham that he'll have myriad children and grandchildren — a sign of favour and prosperity (which you'd need with so many birthday presents). God promised Abraham that his descendants would be as many as the stars in the sky and as many as grains of sand on the shore (Genesis 22:17-18). What God does is seriously productive and fruitful.

We can all be forgetful about things, even about God. When life is good, we tend to breeze along confident in our own ability. When things go wrong, however, we remember God and turn to Him for help. The great challenge of the "God life" is to always remember Him, whether in good times or bad. It's comforting to know that God's people have always been a little forgetful.

There's a phrase that's often repeated in the Bible, "Remember, for the Lord your God..." When things are going badly for the nation of Israel, she's all over God but when things are going well she tends to forget Him. After Israel received the Ten Commandments life was good; in fact life was very prosperous and she was feeling proud of herself. So she needed to be prompted: "But remember the Lord your God, for it is He who gives you the ability to produce wealth" (Deuteronomy 8:18). So, wealth creation doesn't belong to capitalism, it belongs to God. It's He who makes us innovative, product and profitable. God loves money-making entrepreneurship.

The prophet Elijah knew his time in this world had come to an end, so he asked his mentee, Elisha, if there was anything he could do for him before he departed. Elisha, not being shy in any way, asked if he could inherit a double portion of his spirit. To set his expectations, Elijah told Elisha that this would be a difficult thing and that if he saw him depart from this world, his desire would be granted. You can imagine Elisha watching Elijah very closely from that moment forward. It wasn't like he wasn't watching his mentor anyway, but now he would hardly take his eyes off of him. Elisha did indeed see Elijah taken into heaven and he was granted a double portion of Elijah's spirit (2 Kings 2:1-15). God loves the increase and the double!

One of the things that Elisha inherited from Elijah was the care of a community of prophets. One of those prophets had died and his creditors were now pursuing the widow and were threatening to take her sons away. So Elisha asked her what resources she had left and she replied that she only had a small jar of olive oil. Elisha asked her to go and collect empty jars from her neighbours and "don't ask for just a few." The miracle was that the widow's small jar of oil filled every empty jar collected from neighbours. Elisha then told her to sell the oil, pay off her debts and live on what remained — there must have been a lot of oil (2 Kings 4:1-7)! This indeed was a remarkable miracle and demonstration of the productive and generative nature of God.

In the Psalms (1:3), the image of a tree being planted by a river producing fruit and being prosperous is used. Also in Ezekiel (47:12), there's the image of a tree planted by a river producing fruit, not just once, but every month. This is a powerful image of the generative and fruitfulness works of God.

I imagine the name of the business was Simon & Co — a small family-owned fishing company. Simon had learnt the trade from his father and his father's father. One day, a travelling teacher called Jesus, asked to speak to a crowd standing in Simon's boat. As Jesus finished up His talk, He and Simon delved into further conversation: Simon & Co had been fishing all night but had caught nothing. Now, get the irony of this: Jesus the carpenter gives Simon the fisherman advice about how to catch fish. Simon must have had a little chuckle, "What on earth does a carpenter know about fishing?" Frankly, he and his crew had nothing to lose. Simon & Co did as Jesus suggested and threw out their nets and they were full to bursting. So, Simon called out another small business owner on the lake to form a joint venture with them to bring in the catch together. Jesus now proves Himself as a business turnaround expert... how enterprising is that (Luke 5:1-11)?

Most of the stories that Jesus told, were stories about business and commerce, not stories about religion and religious matters. He told stories of farmers, landowners, fishermen, event organisers and winemakers to name just a few. On one occasion, He used the metaphor of a winemaker, describing Himself as the Vine and His Father as the Gardener (John 15:1). He explained that we're like the branches of the vine and that if we remain grafted in the vine, then we'll produce much fruit (i.e. grapes). But if you don't remain in the vine, you'll whither. Like a gardener, God cuts off the parts of the vine that bear no fruit and prunes the parts of the vine that do, so that they can grow and bear yet more fruit: another wonderful picture of the growth and fruitfulness of remaining in God.

A great crowd was following Jesus because of all that He said and did. They must have been doing so for some time because Jesus asked Philip (one of His disciples) how they would eat, in order to test his faith. One of His disciples commented that it would cost a year's salary to buy enough food to feed the crowd. Then a small boy stepped forward offering five small barley loaves and two small fish. I always thought he must've been a very hungry small boy or he came ready to share! Jesus gave thanks for the food and then had it distributed amongst a crowd of five thousand (and that was just counting the men). When everyone had finished eating, the scraps were collected and incredibly, filled twelves baskets (John 6:1-15). Yet another account demonstrating the enterprising and generative nature of God at work.

Jesus told the story of a farmer who went out to sow seed in the field. All the seed was good seed but the ground the seed fell on was pretty inconsistent. Some seed fell on the path and was naturally eaten by birds; some seed fell in rocky places and although it grew when the sun came, it withered and died because it had no roots with which to draw moisture. Other seed fell among thorns and as it grew, it was choked. The seed that fell in good soil grew thirty, sixty and a hundred times (Mark 4:1-8). The farmer must have been delighted with the return on investment: thirty, sixty and a hundred times what he'd planted. God is into business growth and multiplication.

Jesus says the Kingdom of Heaven is like a man going on a journey and entrusting his wealth management to a team. To one, he gave five bags of gold, to another two bags of gold and to another one bag, based on his judgement of their ability to produce him a return whilst he was away. On his return his team reported their return on investment. The man with five bags reported that he had earned five more while the man with two bags had earned another two. The man with one bag reported that he was afraid and had sat on the gold and so returned it in its entirety. Jesus summarises what is meant by the story saying, "For whoever has, will be given more, and they will have an abundance. Whoever does not have, even what he has will be taken from him" *(*Matthew 25:14-30*)*. In the Kingdom of Heaven, it's expected that we take risks and put to work what God has put in our hands. It forfeits who God has asked us to be if we act out of fear, or we're paralysed by fear, and as a result do nothing. Let's allow God to multiply what He's put in our hands.

The story of the early church is sometimes venerated as the ideal model for contemporary church. A slightly blinkered perspective given all the troubles in the early church. As well as the many wonderful and amazing things about the early church, it also had more than its own fair share of disagreements, divorces and divisions! Despite the humanity of the church, and thanks to God's grace, the early church grew rapidly. There's a pattern in the book of Acts that goes like this: about three thousand were added to their number that day (Acts 2:41); and the Lord added to their number daily those who were being saved (Acts 2:47); and the number of disciples in Jerusalem increased rapidly (Acts 6:7). The early church grew incredibly from one-hundred and twenty people at Pentecost to thousands within weeks of its birth. Again, God is about the increase.

There's a clear biblical theme about who God is and what God does. God is an innovative, generative, fruitful, productive, multiplying and increasing God. Kingdom entrepreneurship isn't a "minority sport" to be participated on the margins of faith by a small number of enthusiasts, but it's the mainstream of who God is and what God does. God specialises in taking risks to make a lot out of a little or to create something out of nothing. He is the Great Entrepreneur!

NOTE TO SELF:

I am going to look at God and read the Bible differently; He is the Great Entrepreneur and what He does is enterprising.

Chapter 2

The Mobility of the Kingdom

My First Enterprise

I remember being a teenager and struggling a lot. My "chocolate shop" enterprise was definitely one of my positive memories. Like all teenagers, I was discovering who I was and not making much progress. I remember feeling stupid at school because that's how my teachers made me feel. I remember being very timid and shy. I remember feeling awkward around girls and wondering if I'd ever have a girlfriend. I remember feeling on the fringe of everyone else's friendships. I remember being asked to read the Bible at church and not doing a great job. I remember worrying about what job I'd do when I left school. I remember leaving home at sixteen years old and living in a hostel. I remember being the smallest person in the fifty people recruited into my apprenticeship programme. I remember a lot more and the vast majority of it was wrestling with who I was.

Then, at the age of nineteen, I met some guys who talked about Jesus as if He was with us in the room. They were strange people who made me feel very uncomfortable but there was something undeniably real about what they experienced. Whilst I struggled a lot, I decided to give Jesus a go and we're still on the adventure today.

Discovering that God loved me was really amazing. At this stage in life my dad never told me he loved me. It always felt like my dad could love either my sister or he could love me, but for some strange reason I still don't understand why he could never love us both at the same time. Experiencing that God loved me unconditionally without strings attached, was mind blowing.

There was something more transformational than knowing that God loved me: it was knowing that God liked me and that was life changing. God likes Matt. God likes the way Matt looks. God likes the way Matt thinks. God likes the way Matt feels. God likes Matt's talents. God likes Matt even though he messes up. God likes Matt when he's OK. For me, being liked by God was even more profound than knowing God loved me.

So what was the result of being both loved and liked by God?

I started loving and liking myself. As a result, I started loving and liking other people more. I began growing in personal confidence — if God likes me, does it really matter what anyone else thinks? So, I started making friends with everyone I met.

I joined a global community called "the church" that's present and active in every country in the world. I began to meet incredible people, doing incredible things, in incredible places. My global network exploded. I became hungry to learn and improve myself every day for the rest of my life.

I sensed that God had a special purpose for my life. My motivation, determination and resilience dramatically increased. I started asking more questions about what the right and wrong thing to do in any situation was. My moral and ethical framework was strengthened.

I embarked on a journey of discovering what I believed, were my God-given superpowers. My sense of my own value, worth and significance went through the roof. I started living my life following the example of Jesus and how He treated the people around Him. I became a better person.

So what happens to a person who becomes more comfortable in his/her own skin and who's more confident around others? What happens when someone's connected to a global community of diverse relationships or committed to self-development and experiences a heightened sense of life purpose? What happens to someone who becomes honest with a stronger ethical code and appreciation of his/her superpowers? Do prospects in one's life begin to increase or reduce? Are such people more likely to be selected for promotion at work? Are they more likely to thrive in informal and formal education? Are they more likely to encounter new opportunities? Yes, yes, yes, yes and yes!

Mobility

So, who were you before you encountered Jesus? What has changed in your life since that time? Our lives are transformed as a result of the Kingdom of Heaven. The difference isn't limited to going to heaven when we die but rather about heaven on earth whilst we live. As a result of God's Kingdom, our life prospects and social mobility are transformed.

The British government's Social Mobility Commission says, "Social mobility refers to the link between our starting point in life and where we end up. When our starting point strongly determines where we end up, mobility is low. But if people from all starting points and backgrounds have a good chance of achieving any outcome, then mobility is high." Social mobility is not about what we achieve but what we achieve compared to where we started, otherwise known as distance travelled.

My experience is that encountering Jesus and pursuing the Kingdom of God has dramatically transformed my social mobility. I am not defined by where I started in life. Thanks to Jesus, I'm a new person and my prospects in life have been transformed. This is true for everyone who meets Jesus — they experience the mobility of the Kingdom of God!

The impact on a community of encountering Jesus is massive mobility. Jesus was walking towards a village and as He did, a group of men called out to Him. The ten men had been diagnosed; not by a doctor but by a priest. They had leprosy which, in those times without modern medicine, could lead to painful and disfiguring sores. To prevent the spread of the disease, the lepers were immediately separated from their families and ostracised from their community by forcing them to live in a ghetto outside of their village.

So when the ten men who had leprosy called out to Jesus and He walked across to talk to their community, he broke the rules. Jesus told them to go back to the priests and as they went, they were healed. Only one of the ten men returned to thank Jesus (Luke 17:11-19).

Social Inclusion

By healing the lepers, Jesus socially included them. He was enabling people who had been socially excluded to be socially connected again. The Bible doesn't tell us where the nine healed men went, but I have a theory.

Sometimes I travel overnight, or for a weekend and, occasionally, for a week. I remember the years when my three children were younger. On returning from a trip, I'd turn the key in the door and I'd hear a voice shouting, "Daddy's home!" Then came the noise of feet running down the corridor. My youngest son was always first and then there was the moment when the noise of feet running had stopped because he'd launched himself into the air. He flew through the air and threw his arms around me, hugging tight. My daughter came soon after: she came running down the corridor and reached her arms around my tummy and squeezed me saying in the cutest of voices, “It's so good to see you, Daddy.” Then my eldest son, who was already "too cool for school," walked down the corridor and bumped shoulders saying, "Good to see you, Dad." If you travel away from home, you'll know what it's like to miss your kids!

The Bible doesn't tell us how long the community of ten lepers had been separated from their children. It was most likely more than weeks and months; it was probably years. So, I think I know where those men went when the priest declared them clean, don't you? I think Jesus knew too.

I remember sitting on a red London bus one afternoon next to an elderly lady. I started a conversation and, because it was December, I asked, "Are you looking forward to Christmas?" Suddenly, she became silent. In that moment, I knew why. She was one of the five hundred thousand elderly people who spends Christmas Day alone each year in the UK.

You don't need to be elderly and to live alone to feel isolated and lonely. You can be in a marriage and feel all alone in the world. You can be in a dynamic church and sit there week after week feeling all alone in the world. You can be the life and soul of the party and yet feel all alone in the world. For whatever reason, there are times in our lives when we all feel excluded and alone.

Well there's good news, my friends. God is in the business of social inclusion. The Bible says that God is always with us (Matthew 28:19), that He puts the lonely in families (Psalm 68:6) and gives us the ministry of reconciliation (2 Corinthians 5:18). This is good news; literally good news. Only comfortable Christianity can afford for the Gospel to be about spiritual salvation alone.

Economic Empowerment

By healing the lepers, Jesus also economically empowered them. Separated from their families, community and workplaces, they were unable to earn anything. Each and every day they lived wondering where they would find the next scrap of food. The most likely source of food was probably the village rubbish heap. I can imagine every day, either very early or very late after the villagers had dumped their refuse, the lepers would search the rubbish heaps looking for scraps of food.

Not only were the lepers wrestling with hunger, but they also knew that their families were, too. They'd have been the main income earner in their family, but not any longer. So, each and every day, their families were begging and relying on the generosity of others to survive.

By healing the ten lepers Jesus also economically empowered them. They no longer needed to scrap for food and imagine their families begging. Now they could work for a living. Now, they could return to their workshops and make goods or head to the fields to sow seed and reap a harvest. They could go to the village market to trade goods and services. Encountering Jesus was seriously good news!

At the time of Jesus, there was no government welfare system, it operated as much as Africa does today where there was a family welfare system. If life was tough, you hoped that someone in your wider family was doing well for themselves and that they'd look after you.

I remember sitting in a lounge with a friend in Africa and asking them what was going on: a stream of people were sitting outside an office asking to see a particular person. They'd discretely talk and then seemed to negotiate and some cash would change hands. They explained to me that this was what they call the "black tax:" an expectation that if you're doing well you'll cover the essential costs for others in your family such as education, medical and living costs.

The family welfare system is powerful, but it falls down when no one in your wider family is doing well or if you're estranged from them for some reason. The people Jesus met who were begging for a living, had fallen through the gaps within the family welfare system. So, every healing miracle of Jesus was actually an act of economic empowerment. Jesus was giving people the ability to work again.

I don't know if you've ever experienced a period of unemployment. I have. It was only for six months but many people experience it for much longer. I found it crushing. The cash shortage was certainly a challenge but what was worse than the loss of income was the loss of dignity. Being workless was humiliating and it slowly but certainly erodes and destroys your self-worth. So, imagine being given the opportunity to work again: it not only gives you an income but restores your dignity and self-worth.

The disciples of Jesus, Peter and John, were walking to the temple to pray. A man who had been lame since birth was at the temple gate begging. When he saw Peter and John, he asked them for money. They both looked at him and Peter said, "Silver or gold I do not have, but what I do have I give you. In the name of Jesus

Christ of Nazareth, walk." Peter took him by the hand and helped him up and his feet and ankles became strong and he walked. He immediately went into the temple walking and jumping and praising God (Acts 3). This is seriously good news. Like every healing miracle of Jesus, this was an act of economic empowerment. Someone who begged for a living, was given the opportunity to work for a living, not only to provide for themselves, but also for their family and to be generous to others and regain their human dignity.

Economic empowerment is not some get-rich-quick ideology, or what is sometimes called the "prosperity" gospel, where the only person who actually prospers is the pastor. Without naming anyone, there are many examples around the world where preachers teach prosperity, invite their listeners to donate as a sign of their belief that God will out-give them and then fly around the world in private jets whilst their followers continue to live in poverty. Economic empowerment is quite different to the prosperity gospel: it provides a tangible hope for today that God can help a person enterprise and earn a living to feed their children.

When your ethnic community is over-represented amongst those who are unemployed or in low paid jobs, knowing that you are going to heaven when you die doesn't help feed your children! When your community is over-represented within the criminal justice systems, mental health system and faces unrivalled health inequalities, knowing you're going to heaven when you die makes no difference. Only middle class Christianity can afford for the Gospel to be about spiritual salvation alone.

Missiologists have observed what they call, "redemption and lift:" that when people follow Jesus they become more socially and economically mobile. They criticise this phenomenon because it continually grows a middle class Christianity that finds it difficult to reach the working classes. As I explained earlier, when someone follows Jesus they become more motivated, purposeful, relational, determined and value-driven with a stronger ethical framework. This is actually the mobility of the Kingdom of God.

Political Justice

Jesus' healing of the ten lepers was also an act of political justice. If you define politics as the way we choose to live together as a society, then everything Jesus said and did was political. Jesus talked in public with Samaritans when the Jews hated them, Jesus healed people on the sabbath whilst religious leaders condemned it, He made friends with tax collectors who were despised by others in the community. The list goes on and on.

For years, I was taught that Jesus was a spiritual leader and the Romans and Jews shouldn't have felt threatened by Him because He wasn't a political leader. I've been taught that the

Kingdom of God is spiritual and not political. I now think that's utter rubbish (that's my polite way of saying it). Jesus may not have been a politician or wanted political office but He was extremely political!

Jesus challenged the political injustices of His day. A woman was about to be stoned in the street by a group of men because she'd been caught in adultery. There are so many issues about this! One of my questions is: if she was caught in adultery, where was the man she was caught in adultery with? What sort of society lets the man slip out of the back door whilst the woman is dragged out of the front door to be stoned? What sort of society would allow men to punish a woman in this way?

So Jesus called them out and challenged the men, "Let any one of you who is without sin be the first to throw a stone at her." Immediately, the crowd began to disperse, the older and perhaps wiser men were first until Jesus was the only One left.

Jesus said, “Woman, where are they? Has no one condemned you?”

“No one, sir,” she replied.

“Then neither do I condemn you” (John 8:1-11).

Jesus approached this community of lepers who were scorned, removed from their families and forced to live in a ghetto. He talked with the lepers. In other situations he reached out and touched them (Matthew 8:2). What sort of society would diagnose people with a chronic disease and then force them from their loved ones to live in a ghetto?

Jesus was challenging the way that the society of His day chose to live together. A Gospel of the Kingdom of God should do the same today. As followers of Jesus, we don’t have all the answers, we couldn’t run things better and we don’t want our own political party. We can, however, make a contribution to how we choose to live together as a society. So, speak up rather than be silent; be known for what you are rather than what you are against and engage with the political, rather than sit in prayer meetings.

As someone who simply turned up to volunteer at my local political group one weekend, and then was asked to stand in the local election in an unwinnable seat, but then won — trust me, it's easier than you think!

Well-Done not Over-Done

For too long, we've over-spiritualised, over-futurised and over-individualised the Gospel of Jesus Christ and our reading of the Bible. The Kingdom is spiritual but when it's well-done, it includes social, economic and political matters.

The ancient heresy, Gnosticism, teaches that everything material is bad and everything spiritual is good. If we discover the secret knowledge "gnosis" then we can escape from this material world to the spiritual world above. Sound familiar? So much of contemporary

Christian teaching and praxis is over-spiritualised — it's been shaped more by Gnosticism than it has by the Kingdom of God.

The over-futurisation (I know I'm making up words, but it should be in the dictionary because we both know what I mean) of the Gospel is an inblance: God is here today, not one day.

What if following Jesus isn't about going to heaven when we die? What if it's about heaven coming to earth while we live? The direction of heaven in the Bible isn't about us going to heaven but rather heaven coming to earth. It's time to help the church change its understanding of the direction of heaven. Heaven is perfect, we're going to live in heaven with God for eternity, but the location is here, not somewhere else.

Jesus prayed, "Your kingdom come, Your will be done on earth, as it is in heaven." (Matthew 5:10). In his vision, John said, "I saw the Holy City, the new Jerusalem, coming down out of heaven from God" (Revelation 21:2); and "Come, Lord Jesus" (Revelation 22:20). Following Jesus isn't some great escape plan to get us from this world to the next, it's an occupy movement where we see heaven restored on earth. So, embrace the mobility of the Kingdom of God because we're here to stay!

Western culture has too often applied its worldview to the Bible rather than the biblical worldview being applied to our culture. One of the greatest heresies of Western culture is a rampant individualism: that it's all about me and, in terms of faith, all about God and I and His purpose for my life. The biblical worldview is one that's much more collective. God calls families, cities, tribes and nations.

God called Abraham to follow Him and promised that He'd make him a great leader and make him into a great nation.

God called Israel to be a light to the nations. He didn't call her to an exclusive country club or private member's club relationship with Him. Israel was called by God to be a light — a light to the nations, so that other people would look at Israel and ask who her God was and seek to follow Him.

God spoke through the prophet Jeremiah that Israel should, "Seek the peace and prosperity of the city" (Jeremiah 29:7). Again, we understand that we're here to inhabit and influence our cities for good and for God.

Jesus does not tell us to go and make individual disciples. Jesus also tells us to go make disciples of nations (Matthew 28:19)! Our business is more than getting people into Bible studies to help them understand the Bible better — our business is to shape the well-being of nations.

A Gospel of the Kingdom of God that is over-spiritualised, over-futurised and over-individualised is overdone and impotent to change the world! This is why some of the communities and countries that have the highest number of people who claim to follow Jesus and go to Church are some of the places that have the highest levels of domestic violence, gun crime and corruption. As Paul puts it to Timothy: it's an outward form of religion that denies the true power of God (2 Timothy 3:5).

Let's recognise the negative influence of Gnosticism, "going to heaven" theology and Western individualism. Instead, let's embrace the mobility of the Kingdom that brings about spiritual renewal, social inclusion, economic empowerment and political justice in the here and now, and not solely for me, but for us!

NOTE TO SELF

I am going to embrace the mobility of the Kingdom of God and be intentional about creating social mobility pathways that realise heaven on earth.

Chapter 3

Enterprise the Hope of the World

A Global Foundation

'NAYBA' is a global foundation helping churches love their neighbours and transform their neighbourhoods. This foundation is working in twenty countries across four continents to enable the church to come alongside people who are experiencing isolation, desperation and vulnerability.

The story of the foundation began when a British Prime Minister articulated his vision for a society in which every organisation — profit, public and non-profit — and every citizen, took a greater part. He said it should be where the government didn't draw increasing amounts of tax revenue and where there's an expectation to provide more and more services. It should be a whole society that takes responsibility for those who live around it.

To my ears, this sounded like a rather biblical perspective through which we "love our neighbour" (Matthew 22:39), "love one another" (John 13:34) and are our "brother's keeper" (Genesis 4:9). So, I gathered one-hundred Kingdom leaders to discuss the opportunity that such a meta-narrative created for us. That was the seeds of what became 'NAYBA.'

We're now facing a massive hangover, a hangover from the pandemic in terms of the impact on mental health and financial recovery.

Following that geopolitics are now impacting global supply chains resulting in an exaction of the cost-of-living..

The reality is that no national government can ever tax a population enough to fund all the domestic and international welfare programmes required to address hardship. Nor can charities fundraise enough to run the required welfare programmes that enable people to escape hardship, let alone do what some are claiming about "ending poverty." Only enterprise can bring about deep and lasting change in the midst of these economic challenges.

Enterprise: The Hope of the World

It was once said that local church is the hope of the world. I believe that enterprise is the hope of the world. You can give a person a fish and it will feed them for a day but teach a person to fish and you can feed them for life. Only enterprise creates jobs that permanently lifts people, families and communities out of poverty. Only enterprise can grow micro and macro economies that build and rebuild nations.

In reality, neither the local church nor enterprise are the hope of the world. Jesus is the Hope of the world; however He does choose to use local church and enterprise as agents of the Kingdom of God. The phrase, however, is meant to be provocative and elevates the role of enterprise (and church) in God's coming Kingdom.

Professor Lesslie Newbigin said, "the local church is the hermeneutic of the Gospel," by which he meant that it's the local church that incarnates and translates the Gospel of the Kingdom of God and makes it tangible for real people in real communities. The church is unquestionably a primary agent of the Kingdom of God.

Enterprise is also a critical agent of the Kingdom of God. In countries where religious freedom is limited due to secularisation or outlawed due to persecution, enterprise has freedom to be and do what the local church wouldn't be able to. Even beyond those points, there are things that enterprise can do that other agents can't. Enterprise creates jobs, provides dignity and produces income which, in turn, drives local and national economies. Jobs enable people to buy food that supports local food producers, housing that supports local builders, education that supports local teachers and health care that support local health care workers. Jobs pay taxes which feeds the national economies. What is there not to like about enterprise?

We all have a role to play in encouraging entrepreneurs and enterprise, whether a politician, educationalist, charity leader, church leader or parent. Together, these form part of our enterprise ecosystem that make it easier, or more difficult, to be an entrepreneur and start an enterprise. I'd like to take some time to explore the role of each of these agents in encouraging enterprise and creating this enterprise friendly ecosystem.

The Role of Government

Government is a key to encouraging entrepreneurs and an enterprise-friendly ecosystem. Governments of every political persuasion around the world should be doing more to encourage enterprise. Even in the UK, where there is a positive culture towards enterprise, there are still complicated taxes, countless thresholds and confusing restrictions that are hugely discouraging for entrepreneurs trying to launch new ventures.

Governments should simplify tax systems, provide support from worklessness to new business and get out of the bloody way! Sadly, in many jurisdictions, governments become brakes and barriers rather than accelerators and incentive-givers of enterprise.

The more enterprises start and succeed, the more jobs are created and the more families are lifted out of poverty. As a result, less government welfare is required and the more tax revenues are generated for government — happy days!

Government welfare is absolutely essential for those who essentially need it but for many people, it'll help them get their dignity back. So, we should help them get a job, or help them create a job that is theirs, that belongs to them, enables them to provide for themselves and for their loved ones and so, they can be generous to others.

As someone currently domiciled in the UK, please could the British government become a more enterprise-friendly ecosystem?

The Role of Education

Education is a key to encouraging entrepreneurs and an enterprise-friendly ecosystem.

In my opinion, formal learning prepares you for a job but informal learning prepares you for enterprise. Traditional school education prepares you for a lifetime of doing what you're told and when you're told to do it, which is fine if a series of jobs is what you want out of life. Informal learning teaches you what you need to know to become an entrepreneur: it's through enterprise books, courses and coaching, such as those in which you discover the secrets of launching your own enterprise, creating your own job and being your own boss. Now I admit it's not for everyone but, currently, education is a sausage machine producing people for jobs.

Sadly in many places, education completely misses the opportunity to encourage entrepreneurs, because it's designed, delivered and reviewed by people who aren't entrepreneurs.

As mentioned at the start of this book, I didn't do well at school. I was in remedial English classes and left believing I was stupid because that's what most of my teachers told me. In reality, I wasn't stupid — I'm dyslexic. But when the education system is designed, governed and reviewed by people who think their way of learning is the right and only way, that's what you get.

Most educationalists have the cheek to describe dyslexia as a "learning disability" or a "learning difficulty." In reality, dyslexia is a "learning difference." There's nothing wrong with being dyslexic, but there is something wrong with the system that's so archaic, biased and oppressive.

Dyslexia is a superpower. Personally, I experience the ability to think super-fast, make unusual connections between ideas and people, solve problems visually and speak publicly without notes. A surprisingly high percentage of the world's most successful entrepreneurs, struggled at school because they didn't fit the mould and have a learning difference of some sort.

It's time for formal education to stop being a sausage machine which, regardless of the raw materials you start with, end up with a uniform result. Instead, let's nurture the uniqueness of every human being to be the best they can be in the world. Let's recognise learning differences and create education systems that truly embrace cognitive diversity.

The Role of Charity

Charity is a key to encouraging entrepreneurs and an enterprise-friendly ecosystem.

Food banks are one of the best examples of charity in communities today, but they will never solve poverty. Food banks provide emergency food for a few days in order to get a person or family through a sticky patch. So, more food banks are most certainly not the solution to the global cost-of-living crisis. Only enterprise can do that.

Charities are strong at emergency aid, whether that's domestic or international, but it doesn't solve poverty. Sadly, charity efforts are often limited to meeting immediate needs rather than going upstream to deal with the root causes of problems. Also, any enterprise work they're involved in, is focused overseas. However, I believe that things may be about to change.

Charities also invest in development, facilitating education of children and adults with essential life skills that create the platform for a better future. Again, is this education preparing people for a job or rather to create their own jobs?

Charities are often also involved in advocacy. They work with governments to address structural issues of injustice where legislation has unintended negative consequences for those who are doing life.

It's interesting that international charities often described as NGOs (Non-Governmental Organisations) use enterprise in the developing world but not in their own markets or in their funding countries. NGOs have used programmes to encourage people to start an enterprise that can provide them with a livelihood. In addition, micro-finance has been used extensively as a way of providing capital to start and scale an enterprise. This same approach hasn't, however, been used in their home markets or in the markets of their funding countries where cost-of-living crises may exist. I think this is a major growth opportunity.

The Role of Church

Church is key to encouraging entrepreneurs and an enterprise-friendly ecosystem.

Sadly, over the years the church has struggled to support people in their workplace, let alone entrepreneurs. The sacred secular divide and being in "full-time ministry" thinking, while entrepreneurs' roles are neglected, is still not benign — it's a pervasive theology in the life of the church that damages and destroys its effectiveness in the world.

The Bible is clear that, "The earth is the Lord's,

and everything in it" (Psalm 24:1) and "Whatever you do, work at it with all your heart, as working for the Lord, not for human masters" (Colossians 3:23). It's exhausting to have to go over this again and again, but we'll have to, until we've removed the church of this pervasive theological cancer: the sacred secular divide. We're all full-time for Jesus in whatever we do!

The Bible is also very clear that church leadership gifts are given in order to equip people to be effective in their workplaces. The Apostle Paul writes to the Church in the city of Ephesus, "So Christ Himself gave the apostles, the prophets, the evangelists, the pastors and teachers, to equip His people for works of service, so that the body of Christ may be built up" (Ephesians 4:11-12). The role of church leaders isn't to attempt to control people, but to equip people for works of service.

So, how do church leaders get behind businesspeople? There are lots of ways:

- Preach about business from the Bible. The leaders we preach about were marketplace leaders, not religious leaders: Abraham was a shepherd, Joseph was a prime minister, Esther was a queen, Nehemiah was a sommelier, Simon was a fisherman, Paul was a tentmaker and Aquila was a seamstress. Jesus was a carpenter and all the stories He told were about the workplace: a landowner, a farmer, a shepherd, a winemaker, a tax collector. So let's preach it!

- Teach an integrated biblical worldview (Colossians 1:15-20). Demolish any sacred secular divide especially language of a "secular job" or "full-time ministry." Language creates culture and, sadly, this language has created a strong culture of them and us, spiritual and unspiritual, godly and godless.

- Tell the stories and testimonies of businesspeople from platforms, broadcasts and publications. Have businesspeople tell their stories. Remember, entrepreneurs can end poverty whereas the governments we support and charities we promote are unable to.

- Pray for businesspeople, and all people in the workplace. They're on the frontline and blurry line of the Kingdom of God. It's they who need our prayers, prophecies and encouragement.

- Set up a business group in your church or network of churches. Create a place and a space where businesspeople can encourage one another, pray for one another and help one another.

As we'll explore in the next chapter, churches can ask their business leaders to run 'The Spirit of Enterprise' course, for which they're eminently qualified, in order to help people facing financial hardship start an enterprise. That enterprise could become their main income or a side hustle alongside a job in order to help make ends meet through the global cost-of-living crisis.

So how does your church see entrepreneurs and enterprise as a fundamental strategy of the mission of God?

The Role of Family

Family, and in particular parenting, is a key to encouraging entrepreneurs and enterprise.

Loving unconditionally is the key responsibility of parenting but after that role modelling has to be top of the list. Children take little notice of what we say and notice more what we do. Girls want to know how to be a woman and boys want to know how to be a man. Girls want to know how to relate to men while boys want to know how to interact with women. At some point, they're also going to want to explore what to do with the rest of their lives and again they'll be looking at us. So what are we role modelling to our children about getting a job, or creating a job?

Most people get a job rather than create a job and there's nothing wrong with that! Remember, though, that this has an influence on children. If they see their parents with a job, that's what they'll think is normal and instinctively want to do that. There are a number of things that a parent can do to encourage the spirit of enterprise in their children:

- Make sure your children know people within your wider family and friends who are entrepreneurs and have created jobs for themselves. This might just be the permission given or spark of inspiration necessary.

- Feed the interests and passions of your children. It doesn't mean they'll create a business about that thing but they'll feel happier, be more motivated and it'll feed their productivity.

- Keep formal education in perspective: it's easy to fall into the trap of thinking if a child struggles at school, they're going to struggle in life. That's simply not true. Encourage them to do their best and if school doesn't work for them, it's fine!

- Encourage your child to start a small business around something they're passionate about. My daughter loved art and began making greetings cards. So, I encouraged her and her friend to start a greetings card business from which they made good money as teenagers.

Some communities in which I've worked face the challenge of absent fathers and male role models within family life and home. Boys and young men in this context are particularly vulnerable to finding their male role models elsewhere, even among local gangs who wear aspirational clothes, drive aspirational cars and attract aspirational girls.

So let's build enterprise-friendly ecosystems that encourage and support entrepreneurs and enterprise. Let's not kid ourselves: government, education, charity, church and family cannot solve the cost-of-living crisis. Only enterprise can do that.

NOTE TO SELF

I'm going to build enterprise-friendly ecosystems that encourage entrepreneurs, enterprise and job creation to end poverty.

Chapter 4

Becoming a Kingdom Entrepreneur

A First Rental Property

For the first thirty years of my working life, I was involved in pioneering non-profit work. As a result of this, I had no traditional pension arrangement. I'd been aware of this situation for years but never knew quite what to do. Then, as I began to progress into my fifties, I had a sense that it would be wise to do something!

One day, a French friend and his Italian wife told me about a property they had purchased in Noto, Italy, and asked if I'd like to buy one also. I declined explaining that I didn't have the cash to do so. The next time I heard from them they explained that they'd found me a property! I could immediately see the potential of what I was looking at but, as I was about to explain to them that I still didn't have any spare cash, I stopped myself and began wondering "what if?"

What if I could somehow raise the cash? What if the property could be fully refurbished? What if the property could be a holiday rental? What if the income could be used to pay back the cash? What if, over time, it could be an asset I owned to produce an income?

Noto is the pinnacle of baroque architecture in Sicily. It's close to the sea with some of the finest beaches in the whole of Italy. Sicily is the largest island in the Mediterranean with an incredible sunny climate to match. As the largest wine-producing region in Italy, it's renowned countrywide for its local cuisine. Combined with incredible layers of history, architecture and culture, what is there not to love? The perfect location for a holiday rental!

Given its rooftop view of the city of Noto, I named the home "The Rooftop" and launched it for holiday rental bookings the following year. During each of my visits, I made notes of the best restaurants, beaches, walks, vineyards, artisan and places of interests. I also took lots of photographs with my iPhone. Before I knew it, I realised I have the makings of a full colour travel guide to Noto, Italy. So I pulled together "Matt's Noto: Your guide to one of Sicily's greatest cities" and published it as the holiday rental was launched to market.

What I didn't expect is that people who saw me do all this asked if I could help them buy, develop and manage a property in Noto. What began as a pension asset producing a relatively passive income has turned into a portfolio of holiday rentals.

Oh, by the way, I stumbled across the web domain that I couldn't believe was still available at an affordable price: NotoItaly.com

As this adventure got underway, I accepted that God was an entrepreneur and His spirit of enterprise existed in me, as I believe it does in you! So would you like to become a Kingdom entrepreneur? If so, there are three steps I'd recommend you begin with.

Step 1:
Ask for the God-Given Gift of Enterprise

We can all be forgetful. There are times when we're prone to forgetfulness when life is good. We enjoy our comforts and are thankful about how well we've done. Then, there are the times when life doesn't go so well. In those moments, we cry out in desperation to God for His help. In the good times, it's easy to forget God. If it's any comfort, Israel was just the same: when life was good, the nation could become proud, and when life was tough, it cried out to God. There is a phrase that appears again and again within the Bible: "Remember the Lord your God." That was simply because when life is good, God's people have an inclination to forget Him.

Remembering God is so important. Following the giving of the ten commandments, God said, "Hear, Israel, and be careful to obey so that it may go well with you and that you may increase greatly in a land flowing with milk and honey, just as the Lord, the God of your ancestors, promised you. These commandments that I give you today are to be on your hearts. Impress them on your children. Talk about them when you sit at home and when you walk along the road, when you lie down and when you get up. Tie them as symbols on your hands and bind them on your foreheads. Write them on the doorframes of your houses and on your gates" (Deuteronomy 6:4-9). Then later: "Fix these words of Mine in your hearts and minds; tie them as symbols on your hands and bind them on your foreheads. Teach them to your children, talking about them when you sit at home and when you walk along the road, when you lie down and when you get up. Write them on the doorframes of your houses and on your gates" (Deuteronomy 11:18-20). These are such beautiful words that speak to us about remembering God.

I love the way we're encouraged to remember God all the time: in the everyday, in all our comings and goings of life. The Jewish tradition uses a Mezuzah (meaning "doorpost") which is a piece of parchment on which is inscribed the words of Deuteronomy, above, and contained in a decorative case. The Mezuzah is attached to the doorpost of the house and you touch it on entering and on leaving to remind you of God.

It wasn't long after the revealing of the ten commandments that Israel was already feeling ever so slightly comfortable and smug, and so had to be reminded: "Remember the Lord your God, for it is He who gives you the ability to produce wealth"

(Deuteronomy 8:18).

Wealth creation doesn't belong to capitalism — it belongs to God! Wealth creation is God's gift to give and as we're encouraged, if we'd like something, we should ask for it. "Ask and you will receive, seek and you will find, knock and the door will be opened to you" (Matthew 7:7).

The first step of being an entrepreneur is to ask God for His gift of entrepreneurship. So pause right now and remember, pray and ask for the God-given gift of entrepreneurship.

Step 2:

Believe in Yourself

Whether you think you can or whether you think you can't, you're probably right. Our minds are extremely powerful: if we tell ourselves we can't do something, it'll probably be the case. If we tell ourselves we can do something, that'll probably be the case as well.

One of the graduates from my 'Writing My Book' course said, "I never thought I could write a book, let alone do so in one-hundred days. Now I'm asking what else I've told myself that I can't do, that I actually can."

There was the moment when my friends told me they'd found the perfect apartment for me in the city of Noto in Sicily, Italy. I told myself, for the second time that I couldn't buy it because I didn't have the cash. Then I stopped myself. Maybe I didn't have the cash in the bank or under my mattress but where could I raise the cash?

Normal life raises obstacles and if we can't navigate them by going around, underneath, over the top or simply demolishing them, we won't get very far. If that's normal life, how much more is an entrepreneurial life going to throw up obstacles and barriers?

I remember catching up over lunch with a friend, Paul. We met regularly, but on this occasion I'd a big life decision I wanted to ask his advice about. I explained the choice I was facing and then he said something so profound, that I'll never forget it: "Matt, I believe in you and will support you whatever you decide to do." It was liberating to go out into the world knowing that whatever I did, Paul and other true friends like him would back me.

In the academic paper 'A New Look at Social Support: A Theoretical Perspective on Thriving Through Relationships,' the authors Brooke Feeney and Nancy Collins explore the relationships that enable us to thrive. They identify relationships that are "sources of strength" that enable us to thrive through difficulty and "relational catalysts" that enable us to thrive in opportunity.

The paper is summarised by saying, "Individuals who are supported in these ways are likely to be happy and healthy, confident in their abilities, self-reliant and bold in their explorations of the world, effective citizens who are unlikely to break down in adversity, active contributors to society, sympathetic and helpful to others, and capable of maintaining healthy and prospering relationships. They will not merely survive, but they will thrive, and they will do so with some passion, some compassion, some humour, and some style."

Having someone who believes in you, gives you the confidence to go out into the world and take risks knowing there is somewhere safe for you to return to. Whether that is to cry and recover or to celebrate and laugh with, this is the power of having someone who believes in you and often someone who believes in you more than you believe in yourself.

The second step to being an entrepreneur is believing in yourself!

Step 3:
Call Yourself an Entrepreneur

Words are powerful! James says, "When we put bits into the mouths of horses to make them obey us, we can turn the whole animal. Or take ships as an example. Although they are so large and are driven by strong winds, they are steered by a very small rudder wherever the pilot wants to go. Likewise, the tongue is a small part of the body, but it makes great boasts" (James 3:3-5). This part of the Bible is often used to challenge the words we use about others, but it equally applies to the words we use about ourselves. The words we use about ourselves reflect our heart and mind.

One of God's habits is changing people's names at significant turning points in their lives because names are so powerful. What we call ourselves, what others call us and, most of all, what God calls us, really matters. For example, Abram became Abraham, meaning "father of many" — to signify that God would make one man into a great nation (Genesis 17:5). Simon became Peter, meaning "rock," to signify that it was on his faith that Jesus would build His church (Matthew 16:18). Saul become known as Paul, his Roman name (Acts 13:9), to signify God taking him into the wider world. Our name and the descriptor of who we are really matters.

I've always called myself a non-profit leader and resisted calling myself an entrepreneur. My sense was that calling myself an entrepreneur might give the wrong impression, that I'd made lots of money or achieved great success, which in my eyes I had not. So I never used the name to describe myself.

The reality is that I've initiated or supported start-up non-profit ventures all my life: Joshua Generation, mentoring young leaders; Soul in the City, mobilising thousands of young people in community projects and NAYBA, helping churches love their neighbour and transform their neighbourhoods — to name only three.

During the pandemic, I launched three businesses, Rebottling, providing immersive food and wine experiences; PublishU, coaching people to write, publish and market their books to the world and Noto Italy, helping people rest or invest in the city of Noto in Sicily, Italy. The latter two of these businesses are still thriving and growing today.

In the last year, I've decided that I need to own the name entrepreneur, to signify that I'll start, scale and sustain numerous enterprises. All my life, I've created something out of nothing or made a lot out of a little, reflecting the essence of my God in whose likeness He made me. When I start calling myself an entrepreneur, I discovered a flow and flourishing in this God-given gift that I'd not known before.

So is it about time you started calling yourself an entrepreneur? This is the third step of being an entrepreneur.

Step 4:
Develop Entrepreneurial Habits

So, you've asked for the God-given gift of entrepreneurship and you now call yourself an entrepreneur but now what? It's time to behave more like an entrepreneur. There are seven entrepreneurial habits that I've created for myself. They're not an exhaustive list of habits or form a comprehensive system, but they're habits that I've found to be profoundly valuable to me. So, I share them with you in that spirit.

Habit 1:
Love God and do what you like

Asking, "So what does God want me to do?" is a great question; however, in my mind God has already told us what to do. The Bible is full of what He wants us to do, which is helpfully summed up in Matthew 22:38-39: "Love God and love your neighbour as yourself." My view is that we should avoid sitting around wondering what God wants us to do next and focus on expanding our time, energy and resources doing what He has already told us to do. In doing so, remain open to any further and specific instructions.

There are two ways to view the will of God. The first is using the metaphor of a tightrope. People imagine that there is one way that God wants them to go and if they deviate from it to the left or right, there are serious consequences of potentially eternal significance. This view of the will of God leads people to think in very black and white terms and can result in decision paralysis wondering and waiting for God to "speak" before doing anything else. In my mind, that's no way to live for God.

The alternative way to view the will of God is with the metaphor of an adventure park. You can walk and run, play and explore, and enjoy all the goodness of what has been created. There are some fenced off areas, but you know they're only there to protect you from harm. You're free to live and choose how you'll live.

Which view of the will of God sounds more life-giving to you? Which is more biblical?

I'd like to invite you to come with me to the garden of Eden: it's a beautiful place in which God has created man and woman with the mandate to be fruitful and increase. He also gave just one user instruction: You may eat from any of the trees in the garden except this one! The will of God isn't like a tightrope, it's not restrictive nor is it narrow and controlling. God said eat from any tree in the garden except this one. Yes, the will of God is like an adventure park — it's broad and freeing.

Another way of picturing the will of God is like the relationship between a parent and a child. Good parenting encourages children to follow their passions and interests and flourish and thrive in them and then they check-in now and again to make sure everything is OK. Poor parenting wants to control children and tell them what to do and what not to do all the time.

I live by the mantra "love God and do what you like." If we love God with all our heart (Matthew 22:37) and our minds are renewed by Christ (Romans 12:2), then we are completely free to do what we like. This approach to life is truly life-giving and creates space for entrepreneurialism.

Habit 2:
Embrace uncertainty, ambiguity and risk

Not knowing is one of the hardest and most uncomfortable experiences in life.

Many people combat feelings of uncertainty by pursuing certainty. Within faith communities, the pursuit of certainty is one of the factors that leads to fundamentalism, dogmatism and Neo-Gnosticism. Some Christians are not trinitarian but are quadritarians: they worship the Father, the Son, the Holy Spirit and the Bible. They are "biblioratorists" who often idolise the leaders that expound the Bible for them.

The reality is that faith and enterprise are full of paradoxes, mystery and uncertainty. The book of Hebrews says, "Now faith is confidence in what we hope for and assurance about what we do not see" (Hebrews 11:1). The antidote to uncertainty isn't certainty, but rather faith and hope.

When I was presented with the property investment opportunity, my first reaction was negative. But when presented with it a second time, I began to wonder: could I take the risk to raise the money I didn't have, to make this work? There would be so many unknowns, but why not? I was never going to create something out of nothing or a lot out of a little if I only lived in the place of certainty and minimal risks.

Being an entrepreneur requires an ability to live with uncertainty, ambiguity and risk. There are so many unknowns in starting, scaling and sustaining an enterprise, and there are always more unknowns coming around the corner. So let's get comfortable with discomfort!

Habit 3:
Launch and learn, don't plan and perfect

For me, being an entrepreneur means being willing to launch and learn as you go rather than planning and perfecting before you get off the ground. If you plan and perfect, it's likely that the opportunity will pass or someone else will get there before you. Whereas, if you're willing to launch the venture in a small way and learn and grow, you have immediate forward momentum.

Some of the early church apostles were causing trouble, so they were arrested and kept in jail overnight before being brought to the Sanhedrin the following morning. The apostles claimed that they must obey God, not human beings, at which point the leaders of the Sanhedrin wanted to put them to death. A Pharisee and teacher of the law, Gamaliel, who was honoured by the people, stepped forward and suggested the apostles were put outside for a while. Gamaliel then made the case that the apostles be left alone because if what they were doing was of human origin, it would fail; however if it was from God there is nothing they could do to stop it. The Sanhedrin took his advice and had the apostles released (Acts 5:38-39).

This is what I call the Gamaliel Principle: the best way to find out if something is going to work is to give it a chance and see what happens.

I wrote 'The Spirit of Enterprise' course and book within a couple of weeks and had it published within a month. The book was never going to be a work of literature but could it have been better if I'd spent a year writing it? Yes, it most certainly would have been. But did it need to be better to get this initiative going and enable churches to help people start enterprises? No, it didn't. Sometimes 80 per cent there, is good enough.

In my view, the best thing to do with any idea is to try it and see if it works. If it does work, then scale it up. If it doesn't work, its best to fail fast, call it quits and grab all the learning you can on the way. This is the way of an entrepreneurial leader.

Habit 4:
Relationships are the true currency of business

God is relationship, God is community, God is love. In Genesis chapter one, we see the beginning of the revelation of God as trinity: three in one and one in three. It says, "In the beginning God ... the Spirit of God was hovering over the waters ... And God said." God, His spirit and His word as the revelation of who God is progresses through the Bible. We discover God as Father, Son and as Holy Spirit. One of the powerful metaphors used to describe the holy family of the trinity has been a dance because of the dynamic interaction and interdependence that exists. The Father loves the Son, the Son loves the Father and they send the Spirit into the world to continue their work. Within the community of the trinity there is love, self-sacrifice and preferment of the other — the heart of relationships.

We're told that we're created in the likeness and image of a God of love, relationship and community. Therefore, we're made for love, relationships and community. Whatever our belief system, the reality is that we'll only flourish and thrive in relationship with other people — in our work contexts, among our colleagues, clients and suppliers. This is why I say that relationships are the true currency of business! No matter how many policies, procedures, strategies and systems you have in place, it's trusting relationships that make things work.

So the smart entrepreneur invests heavily in collecting, keeping and growing relationships, because they know that a flourishing and thriving enterprise will result from great relationships.

If needed, there are strong business reasons for treating everyone like a VIP, including the fact that you don't always know who a person is, or who a person knows or who a person will become. However, as I say in my business book 'Relationology,' "The greatest test of our authenticity is how we treat those people who we think can do nothing for us." Don't focus on how to give in order to get from relationships but on how to give in order to grow yourself. This is the core challenge for all our relationships.

The Bible isn't a book about religion, but a book about relationships. It's a book of books, or a book of journals, recording different people's experiences of their relationship with God.

Habit 5:
Pursue the business advantage of diversity

Like attracts like and that's a challenge because if we're only surrounded by people like us, we only have access to the ideas, opportunities and resources that people like us have. If, however, we can develop strong relationships with people unlike us, we have access to the ideas and opportunities that people unlike us have.

Diversity comes in many forms: the most commonly talked about are ethnic and gender diversity. Snowy peak syndrome describes the disproportionate number of white people at the executive level of organisations compared to those of ethnically diverse origins. The top of organisations are also disproportionately male. As I say, like attracts like. But worse than that, they keep it to themselves.

Another completely different arena is that of cognitive diversity: people whose brains and thinking works differently. I am dyslexic, which I have long argued isn't a learning disability or even learning difficultly, but rather a learning difference. My learning difference is a superpower that enables me to think fast, solve problems, make connections and speak publicly without notes.

Diversity is an entrepreneurial advantage so let's ensure that we have diverse partners, diverse suppliers, diverse teams, diverse boards and diverse advisers.

Habit 6:
Build a team who can start, scale and sustain

Teamwork makes the dream work! As an entrepreneur, you have to be able to put your hand to pretty much every responsibility in a business, because when you start it, you are the head of everything. You are head of marketing, sales, business development, service, operations, finance, HR, IT, data and everything else. My experience is that, as an enterprise grows, you're able to grow your team and hire people who are specialists in those areas so that you can focus on what you do best.

The Bible provides us with a powerful metaphor of teamwork when the apostle Paul explains to the church at Corinth, "Just as a body, though one, has many parts, but all its many parts form one body, so it is with Christ ... But in fact, God has placed the parts in the body, every one of them, just as He wanted them to be. If they were all one part, where would the body be? As it is, there are many parts, but one body" (1 Corinthians 12:12, 18-20).

Entrepreneurs who are unable to build a team ultimately fail, because they can't do more than the start-up phase of their enterprise. In fact, an enterprise that's really going to grow never stops "starting up." This ensures that it's always innovating and fresh. It never stops scaling; therefore, it's always growing. It maintains those capabilities alongside its sustainability to ensure that it's long-lasting and enduring.

Habit 7:
Work hard and rest hard

There's no doubt that as an entrepreneur you need to invest everything you have and then a bit more in your venture. That said, there's no point in killing yourself in Jesus' name: you are of little use to anyone as a martyr. As the airplane instructions say, "put your own safety mask on first" and then — and only then — help others do the same. Otherwise, everyone could be a loser!

Jesus made it clear that you can't love your neighbour unless you love yourself (Matthew 22:39). You can't care for your neighbour unless you care for yourself. You can't be kind to your neighbour unless you are kind to yourself.

Life and enterprise aren't a sprint and also not a marathon: it's a lifetime of marathons. So look after yourself and make sure you're in good shape for the long road ahead. My personal mantra is "work hard and rest hard." I can work without ceasing for a long period of time. However, I also recognise that I need space and rest.

There are lots of things that I find restful, restorative and regenerative. I love to walk in deserted places and simply enjoy being. I love to sit or lie in the sun and feel the warmth of the sun on my face and body. I love listening to music whether in my own private world on my headphones or in a live music venue. I love to get lost reading a fiction book or watching a film. Even when I travel internationally, I ensure that I continue to have at least one day off a week in order to pace myself and look after myself. What is it that refills your tanks?

Sometimes it's in the rest that the revelation comes. I often find it's when I'm relaxing, that new ideas or solutions simply come to mind. So, I scribble them down quick to ensure I don't lose them and come back to them later.

These are the entrepreneurial habits that I live by. As I said, they're not an exhaustive list, nor are they a comprehensive model. They're mine and so, as the fourth step of being an entrepreneur, I'd encourage you to either adopt mine or create your own entrepreneurial habits.

NOTE TO SELF:

I've received the God-given gift of entrepreneurship. I believe in myself; I'm an entrepreneur and I'm going to practice entrepreneurial habits.

Chapter 5

The Spirit of Enterprise

The Times Newspaper

As we emerged from the pandemic in 2021, I wrote an article in The Times newspaper in which I called for an outbreak of something more powerful than a virus — an outbreak of the "spirit of enterprise." Little did I realise at the time, but the article and this phrase in particular would define a significant part of the next season of my life. It would also change the lives of many people, churches and communities around the world.

I write frequently for The Times newspaper and always receive encouraging feedback, but on this particular occasion the metaphorical mailbag was enormous. People I knew, people I didn't, people from the UK and people from all around the world took time to write. The energy it created for me was immense.

The following weekend it came to me in a moment: churches need a practical way of helping people in their neighbourhoods who are facing financial hardship to start an enterprise. So I wrote a course, 'The Spirit of Enterprise' that churches could ask their business leaders to run; enabling people who are struggling financially, to start a business. The course naturally flowed. I added some explanations, examples and templates and created a course in a book. The book was published the following month.

It was one of those phone-a-friend moments. I

called Jane Gould who, incredibly, offered to help get 'The Spirit of Enterprise' off the ground. Another friend and church leader, Neal Stanton, offered to be the first to run 'The Spirit of Enterprise' course and four people started an enterprise as a result. Amazingly, The Times newspaper ran a double page spread about what happened and published it in their business section. The book was published in six languages and churches in countries around the world began running the course.

The need for lasting solutions to financial hardship increased following Russia's invasion of Ukraine. Then food and energy prices began escalating and the world experienced a cost-of-living crisis. Now, the world needed something more powerful than an economic crisis: an outbreak of the spirit of enterprise!

'NAYBA' is now enabling churches around the world to run 'The Spirit of Enterprise' course to help people who are struggling financially start a business.

One UK church even purchased a building from which to run 'The Spirit of Enterprise' course and then to provide an 'Enterprise Hub,' offering shared office space and enterprise mentoring for budding entrepreneurs.

So what does 'The Spirit of Enterprise' seven-session course look like?

Session 1:
Transformation not Transaction

Why start an enterprise?

Know your why! As Stephen Covey once said, "Start with the end in mind." Begin every new journey with the end in mind. As you look to start an enterprise, why are you doing it? Is it simply a transaction to generate income? Of course, there's nothing wrong with that! Or do you have transformational aspirations? Would you like the enterprise to create opportunities or jobs for other people? Is the enterprise going to be your main work or is it a side hustle to supplement your main income? Are you building an enterprise to keep in the family or would you like to build it and sell it in five years' time?

For example, I purchased a property in Italy with the motivation to generate a relatively passive income for myself. I had no traditional pension arrangement so buying a rundown property, developing it and then letting it as a holiday rental would create an income for later in life. This is my why.

Session 2:
Innovation not Invention

What are you going to sell?

You don't need to be a mad inventor to be an entrepreneur. You can take an existing product or service and innovate and improve it by ten per cent and it's as if it were a new product or service. What product or service do you have in mind? You may have a mad inventor idea but, more likely, you have an innovation of an existing product or service in mind. Have you had a disappointing experience of a product or service recently that you think could be better?

What is your business model? How are you going to make money? What are the costs to you of delivering the product or service? How much can you charge and what's your margin?

Session 3:
Felt need not Fanciful Passion

Who are your customers?

Every enterprise needs a market or a community of potential customers who are interested in your innovation or invention, because it provides a solution to the felt need they have.

I often meet people, especially in the non-profit world, who are passionate about a particular product or service but it's one hundred per cent personal passion and zero per cent market need. When you ask who their product or service is for, it's for "everyone," because they don't know who their target customer is.

Then, of course, there's the competition. Who are the people offering similar products and services in this space and what can you learn from them? What's different about your product or service? How do you gain a competitive advantage?

For example, I designed 'The Spirit of Enterprise'

course and book to help people start an enterprise, because I saw a felt need. Following the pandemic, and then with the emergence of the global cost-of-living crisis, I saw people who were without work who could help to start an enterprise or who were struggling to make their finances work who could start a side hustle. This is the felt need.

Session 4:
Launch and Learn not Plan and Perfect

When are you starting?

There are two ways to launch an enterprise. You can plan and plan until you think it's close to perfect and then launch. Or you can plan it, launch it and learn from it and continuously improve it. The risk with planning and perfecting your enterprise is that the moment in time could be lost. It's better to simply launch the enterprise and if isn't going to work, find out fast and move on to your next enterprise idea. But if the launch works, then improve and scale as fast as you possibly can! As Nike ads say, "Just do it!"

For example, I first coached a 'Writing My Book' course because I was being asked by so many people for help in writing their own book, so I knew there was a market. I sketched out an eight-session step-by-step course based upon how I write books and then launched it! Each time I ran the course, I made improvements: I wrote a resource which I provided after each session; I moved the sessions around to increase the percentage of people completing their manuscript within a one-hundred days; I moved from a one-off course to starting a course once a term, alternate months and now every month. This is a launch and learn enterprise.

Session 5:
Soul Mates not Solo

Who are your team?

Everyone has superpowers: things that they're better at than the people around them. Given that every strength has a downside, being really good at one thing automatically means that we're not so good at something else. As we explored in the last chapter, if we want your enterprise to flourish and thrive, it means you can't do it solo — you need soulmates. Maybe a 50/50 business partner and/or a team of people with different skills which you'd need in order to enable your enterprise to thrive. Initially, you probably can't afford to salary them, so maybe offer shares, a short-term contract or payment on results.

For example, I'm passionate about the global church being relevant. So in 2019, I launched 'NAYBA' as a global foundation helping churches to love their neighbours and to transform their neighbourhoods. Initially, I was a team of one person. Then, during the first year, Gary joined me, and now we're a team with capacity to continue starting-up, scaling-up and sustaining. These team members are my soulmates.

Session 6:
Size not Share

How big is what we are growing?

Would you rather own one hundred per cent of an enterprise worth one hundred thousand pounds or twenty-five per cent of an enterprise worth one million pounds? Of course, owning a smaller part of a bigger pie is better than owning the whole of a small pie. In the first case, you'd own one hundred thousand pounds, in the latter you'd own two hundred fifty thousand pounds. Which would you prefer?

Can you fund the growth of your enterprise from organic cash flow alone? Or do you need to raise cash by selling shares in order to grow your enterprise?

There are people out there who are experts in venture funding and could help you structure your business, create a pitch deck and raise the necessary funds. So if this is something you'd like to consider best, get some help from someone who knows what they're doing.

Session 7:
Leadership not Limitations

What are we leading?

All leaders have limitations. In the Bible, when God called someone to leadership, they normally responded with a reason why they couldn't do it. Moses said he wasn't confident with words (Exodus 4:10) and Isaiah said he was unclean (Isaiah 6:5). I love this because it's so human, just like you and I!

Leadership has three dimensions: The first dimension is self-leadership. How do you lead yourself? As a leader, it's critically important to invest in your own self-care. You should protect your integrity, keep a sharp mind and fit body, invest in your personal development, manage your relationships well and ensure that you're in an all-round good shape.

The second dimension of leadership is that we lead the business of our business. As a leader, we should constantly build, enhance and improve the delivery of our value-adding products and services. We can't afford to stand still and fail to learn, evolve and transform. The environment is changing and our competition is advancing — there's a constant need to adapt and advance.

Finally, the dimension of organisational leadership: We cannot afford to be so busy working in the business, that we forget to work on the business. It could be strengthening governance through developing the board, growing capacity by recruiting new and diverse team members or preparing end-of-the-year accounts and an annual report. These matters keep the organisation healthy and in a position where it can grow and expand.

Whether large or small, our enterprise has financial, data and people systems and processes that need following in order to remain healthy.

This is an overview of 'The Spirit of Enterprise' course. Who are the businesspeople in your church who might be inspired to run the course to help people start a business that could change their lives and the lives of others?

Enterprise Hub

Churches are encouraged not just to run 'The Spirit of Enterprise' course, but to set up an 'Enterprise Hub' as a co-working space and offer ongoing support to budding entrepreneurs that enables them to succeed.

Churches with buildings often find them sub-optimised throughout the week. Setting up an 'Enterprise Hub' is a powerful way of utilising your building for a great missional purpose. If leadership is lonely, then entrepreneurship can be really lonely. So, having a place where entrepreneurs can work from, such as a shared office space, creates camaraderie and community.

Churches often have business people within their community. This is the perfect opportunity to invite them to use their business skills by mentoring an entrepreneur as they start-up a business. There aren't many people who can't simply give one hour a week to meet an entrepreneur for a coffee to encourage them in their enterprise.

Churches tend to spend a disproportionate amount of their budget on Sunday events. Running an 'Enterprise Hub' provides an amazing opportunity to invest in missional activity through the week. This may include making 'Enterprise Grants' to entrepreneurs to help them get going with their business. A couple of thousand pounds can make the world of difference when you're starting off from scratch.

Churches are full of skilled people. There's the potential to offer support services to help them start-up their business. Maybe there's an accountant in the church who's willing to provide some free advice to entrepreneurs, or a lawyer to offer some free legal advice. There might be a printer who is willing to give a discount on their services. There are myriad possibilities only limited by willingness and creativity.

What could your church's 'Enterprise Hub' look like?

NOTE TO SELF:

I am going to inspire my church to address the cost-of-living crisis by running 'The Spirit of Enterprise' course and setting up an 'Enterprise Hub.'

Chapter 6

My Kingdom Enterprise

A Publishing Company

So, how about launching a Kingdom enterprise yourself? Or if you already have one, why don't you start another, or, perhaps, a side hustle enterprise to work alongside your main thing?

Some time ago I was sitting with a friend and he asked me about the content for some keynote speeches I was delivering at a conference the following week. He immediately said, "Matt, that's a book!" He picked up the telephone and called his publisher and after some pleasantries, he said something like, "I've got a guy here with me that's got a book in him. Will you publish it?"

I'll never forget what happened next: my friend passed me the telephone saying, "Now, tell him about your book." I nearly wet myself! Anyway, that's how I came to publish my first book.

Writing books can become addictive and it certainly has for me. I've now authored more than twenty books. I discovered that once I'd successfully written, published and marketed books, people who wanted to do the same, came to me for advice. I love helping people achieve something new, but the number of people asking for help was getting in the way of my day job.

So, I thought to myself: Why not design a course that takes people step-by-step through the process of writing, publishing and marketing a book? I'd help people in a single group rather than lots of one-on-one conversations and they could pay a little something for the benefit.

Roll forward two years, and I was starting new 'Writing My Book' online courses every month, through which I was coaching people to write their book in one-hundred days. Our publishing house was publishing two books globally every month and we launched a suite of strategic marketing packages to enable our authors to promote their books to the world. That is how www.PublishU.com began!

By the way you need to know that at school I was in remedial English classes. I wasn't allowed to do computer studies, because I was told that my grasp of the English language wasn't good enough. The words of one of my school reports were playing in my head, "Matthew won't come to much!" I was later diagnosed as being dyslexic and my struggles at school began to make more sense. I am, therefore, not your typical author, book coach or publisher, but I think God likes that!

My goal now is to help ten-thousand people acquire the skills they need to write a book. Each book changes at least one life and some books change thousands of lives. Some authors become addicted like me and go on to write multiple books that change even more lives.

Authors have friends and family who themselves will be inspired to write books. One author said, "My ten-year-old son has watched me write and publish a book. Now he thinks it's normal to write a book and has started writing small books himself."

The multiplier effect of this Kingdom enterprise is something that excites me!

So how about launching a Kingdom enterprise yourself? Or if you already have one why don't you start another?

Business Plan

I've never written a traditional business plan in my life but business plans do come in different shapes and sizes! As a cranky Old Testament prophet once said, "Write down the vision and make it plain." (Habakkuk 2:2). There's something about writing down vision and writing down goals that challenge us to be crystal clear about what we want to achieve. Although it might be difficult, the discipline of writing your business plan down is highly valuable.

The only time you might have to write a "traditional business plan" is when you wanted to raise finance from a bank or financial institution. The reality is when you need money, banks won't lend it to you. However, when you don't need money, they want to lend it. Banks hate risk — they want to make money. So, most of the time there's an easier and less risky way to do that than you!

There are other sorts such as the "pitch deck business plan" which is something you would produce if you were running a seed or second stage funding round for a business. It would provide an overview of the business, using great pictures and headline messages.

Then there's a "one page business plan" which is more than sufficient for most other purposes.

I must confess that I mostly work from "beer mat business plans" — relaxing on my own in a bar or when I'm chatting with a friend and I have a flash of inspiration. To ensure I capture the idea, I grab the nearest thing I can write on, which is normally a beer mat, and I scribble away! In fact, in my home I keep beer mats around. They protect surfaces from drinks, but it also means I can grab one and scribble on it!

Enterprise Plan

When I start a new enterprise, there are a number of things that I automatically think through in my head which at some point get translated onto my "Enterprise Plan." Many of these matters are covered in 'The Spirit of Enterprise' book and course but here they are in summary using 'PublishU' as a case study:

- NAME & DOMAIN. What are you going to call the enterprise? The name of my enterprises are often determined by what .com domain name I can secure.

  For example, 'PublishU' was chosen, because I managed to purchase PublishU.com The domain name was available and the name works because it does what it says on the tin.

- WHY. Why are you starting this enterprise and what do you want it to achieve? One of the motivations behind an enterprise is normally to generate money, but not always.

  For example, I've authored twenty books and I know that I can easily write another twenty. However, what is motivating me about 'PublishU' is to help thousands of others acquire the skills to write, publish and market their own books globally. What if I could help ten-thousand people write the book that's inside of them, half of them get published and half of them go on to write other books? Then there's the ripple effect of children growing up in homes where mum or dad has written a book. So, writing a book is normal for those children and they grow up expecting to write a book. This is what motivates me.

- PROBLEM. What pain does your enterprise solve? People are twice as motivated to avoid pain than they are to gain benefit. If you can identify an issue that causes people pain, you're much better positioned for a winning enterprise.

  For example, I meet people who would like to write a book one day but don't know where to start or have started but have got stuck. Then others have written their book but can't get it published. Traditional publishers are notoriously difficult when it comes to securing a contract and they're increasingly asking new authors to buy the first one-thousand books. Self-publishing is an option but if you've never done it before it's fraught with challenges and you could end up with a sub-standard looking book.

- SOLUTION. How does your enterprise solve the problem?

  For example, the 'Writing My Book' online course coaches people over a period of one-hundred days to write their book, with eight out of ten people graduating with a manuscript. The 'Publish My Book' service combines the best of the quality of traditional publishing, with the freedom of self-publishing and adds to that our unique global offer to publish and market your book to the world.

- BIZ MODEL. How does your enterprise make money? What do you charge? What are the costs? How much is the margin?

  For example, 'PublishU' makes money through people paying for the 'Writing My Book' online course through which I coach them how to write their book. The course is delivered online. Therefore, the only costs are my time and some technology. Beyond that, there's margin for the business.

- TARGET CUSTOMERS. Who are the people who would pay for your solution to fix their problem? There's always a temptation to say, "everyone" or to be vague. There's a real power in creating one or more avatars about your typical customer and then target them. You'll find others will tag along and that's fine.

  For example, Target Customers for 'PublishU' are people who lead or own an enterprise, whether it be for profit or not-for-profit. They see the advantage for building their personal and organisational brand by becoming a published author.

- PROMOTION. How are your target customers going to find out about your solution?

  For example, 'PublishU' target customers hear about the 'Writing My Book' course in one of two ways: a) through a workbook, 'My Book Idea,' which is given free to help people develop the concept for their first book; b) through word-of-mouth marketing from people who've become published authors as a result of our services.

- COMPETITION & ADVANTAGE. Who is your competition and what competitive advantage do you have? Every enterprise has competition, so don't kid yourself that yours doesn't.

  For example, 'PublishU' offers 'Publishing My Book' services and its competitors are myriad traditional publishers and self-publishers. Its competitive advantage is its reach, efficiency and cost. The reach of 'PublishU' is global, unlike traditional and self-publishers, which are predominantly home markets. The efficiency of 'PublishU' is its submission of manuscript to publication within three months, whereas it's a minimum of twelve months for traditional publishing and six for self-publishing. The cost of 'PublishU' is two-thirds of self-publishing.

- FINANCIAL PROJECTIONS. What are your cash flow projections for the first twelve months?

  For example, 'PublishU' is aiming to double its revenue in the coming 12 months.'

- RESOURCE REQUIREMENTS. What resources are needed to get the enterprise off the ground and in the air?

  For example, 'PublishU' resource requirements are primarily a growing team of people with the right skills, including management, wordsmiths, copy editors, proof-readers, cover designers, typesetters and marketers.

- KPI. What are your enterprise key performance indicators for the first three, six and twelve months?

  For example, KPIs for 'PublishU' over the next twelve months are to: a) increase the number of courses from one per month to two per month; b) increase our publishing capacity from two books a month to four books a month; c) launch our 'Marketing My Book' services.

You can download "Matt's Two Page Enterprise Plan" template from www.matt-bird.com

First Shoes

I must confess that I like fashion. At least, that's how I explain it! I probably have more pairs of shoes in the wardrobe than the average man. My favourite are a pair that my mum gave me: they're the pair of shoes I learnt to walk in! I love those blue leather Clarks shoes.

The tips of the shoes are scuffed from where I learnt to walk. One shoe took such a battering that the leather has worn through, so there's a hole in the leather. Those shoes remind me that first steps are important no matter how faltering they may be and that the difference between success and failure is the ability to get up and try again.

Whenever I'm struggling with something in life, or with an enterprise, I think about my first pair of shoes. I remind myself that all I have to do in order to succeed is to keep taking steps no matter how small and faltering they may be. Ultimately, success is the sum of small incremental gains! So, if at first you don't succeed, simply try and try again.

When you've dreamt up an enterprise, drafted a two-page enterprise plan and launched, remember that you need to learn to walk before you can run. You're in launch-and-learn phase. Therefore, it'll be a little messy around the edges with many improvements to make — but that's the point! You're building your enterprise in the air and not on the ground!

NOTE TO SELF:

I'm a Kingdom entrepreneur and I'm going to write my plan down.

ENTERPRISE PLAN

NAME & DOMAIN

What are you going to call the enterprise and what is its domain name?

WHY

Why are you starting this enterprise and what do you want it to achieve?

PROBLEM

What pain does your enterprise solve?

SOLUTION

How does your enterprise solve the problem?

MODEL

How does your enterprise make money?

TARGET

Who are the people who would pay for your solution to fix their problem?

PROMOTION

How are your target customers going to find out about your solution?

COMPETITION

Who are your competition and what competitive advantage do you have?

www.Matt-Bird.com

ENTERPRISE PLAN

FINANCIALS

What are your cash flow projections for the first 12 months?

RESOURCE NEEDS

What resources are needed to get the enterprise off the ground?

KPI's

What are your enterprise key performance indicators for the first 3, 6 & 12 months?

www.Matt-Bird.com

Conclusion

In life and in any given situation, we can choose to be a victim or an agent. A victim blames their circumstances, someone else or something else as the reason why they "can't" be, do or achieve something. An agent recognises that they cannot control their circumstances, other people and other things, but they're one hundred per cent in control of themselves and can take charge in any situation.

There are lots of circumstances, people and things that can be blamed for the global cost-of-living crisis: geopolitics, government and greed. However, to linger there, is to behave like a victim.

A poverty mentality focuses on what you don't have rather than on what you do have at your disposal. It perpetuates the current situation, believing there's no way out and that the cost-of-living is rising so fast, that you can never keep up.

There's only one way out of the cost-of-living crisis and that's to take agency; to say that regardless of the external factors, my community is in charge of its own destiny. We're going to start enterprises, generate cash, create jobs, enable families and communities to flourish and thrive.

Let's limit our media intake that feeds a victim and poverty mentality, that polarises communities, promotes extremism, pulls down leaders and tells us how bad things are. Instead, focus on the great entrepreneur who is creative, innovative, generative, productive and fruitful. Let's take agency and allow the spirit of enterprise to grow within us. Let's ask for more of the God-given gift of enterprise and start businesses small and large alike.

About the Author

Matt is a business and social entrepreneur, as well as a global speaker, author and broadcaster.

He has spoken in fifty countries to more than one million people and has authored twenty books. He also writes for publications such as The Times newspaper.

Matt has started numerous business and social ventures which currently include:

- **NAYBA,** a global foundation helping local churches to love their neighbours and transform their neighbourhoods, where he is the Founder.

- **PublishU,** a global venture helping people write, publish and market their books worldwide, where he is the Chief Coach.

- **Relationology,** a global community of great people doing great things through great relationships, where he is the founding Partner.

- **Noto Italy,** a venture helping people rest and invest in the city of Noto in Sicily, Italy.

- **Matt-Bird.com,** a platform inspiring people in faith through his speaking, writing and broadcasting.

When he isn't travelling, he lives between London, United Kingdom and Noto, Italy.

www.CoffeeWithMatt.com

Other Books

Travel

Matt's Noto

Business

Relationology 101

Grow Your Business

Superpowers

Community Transformation

Love Your NAYBA

Transform

The Spirit of Enterprise

Replicate

Civic

Other

Freedom

Visions & Dreams

A Lot with a Little

Elevate

The Relationship Book